Additional Praise for
Prayer for Relief

Prayer for Relief is the representation of turning your pain into beauty. Each poem is achingly intentional, from poetry form to word choices and placement. Krystle does not shy away from the dark fringes of grief and how it takes us on a journey of questioning to resentful acceptance. She tenderly honors the life of her brother with this delicately steeped poetic offering.
—Camari Carter Hawkins, author of *Death by Comb*
and founder of Mama's Kitchen Press

In *Prayer for Relief,* Krystle May Statler takes us into the depths of grief, rage, and loss with intricate poems that clutch at the hem of our sweaters on frigid days. Unafraid of what comes from harboring such pain, each poem stands alone while crashing into one another. This meditation on the loss of a loved one, especially a brother fallen victim to a system bent on burying him, cleaves at our idea of closure—instead, reopens every wound and asks for clean water. A gripping collection not to be dismissed.
—Monica Prince, author of *Roadmap: A Choreopoem*

Like the "Mad Ireland" that Auden says "hurt" Yeats "into poetry," madness "hurt" Krystle May Statler "into" this stunning and heartbreaking tribute to her brother, *Prayer for Relief.* Here is a debut collection that successfully makes sense out of the senseless, to find solace in the inconsolable grief when the one you love so deeply is taken prematurely. Statler brings the horror of gun violence in America directly to her readers as she chronicles the complete and complex life of her brother, BJ. "what was/your favorite ice cream or/did you prefer poetry/over silence or do you miss/Mommy's hugs or Dad's obsession/with Ridgid tools." This is a confrontation that does not point fingers. Instead, *Prayer for Relief* holds hands with each poem so that a change of heart and mind can become a reality for both the reader and the speaker. There are QR codes that once accessed, stare back, haunt, and "hurt" one back into BJ so that he remains cared for in her poems: "To the fallen daffodils, I say he is still here./To the sirens stalking savagely on the narrow/ bridges, he is still here." Hurt arrives in many forms: rage, disbelief, courage. There is no debut book I have read that brings readers along a "hurt" journey with the writer in quite the way Statler has accomplished. *Prayer for Relief* returns us to our own loved ones to keep them forever present.

—**F. Douglas Brown, author of** *Zero to Three,*
winner of the 2014 Cave Canem Book Prize

Prayer for Relief exemplifies what Toni Morrison called the "reach toward the ineffable," the power of attempting to mourn through language, even when language is insufficient. In this collection, Statler responds to her brother's death—and to the ongoing record of fatal shootings by police officers—by posing to us the question of how we might transform bare facts into poetry. Through formal constraints and clever reinventions of familiar texts, Statler talks back to the banalities of legal procedures, autopsy reports, prayers, and everyday speech, and invites playfulness into even this unfathomable loss. *Prayer for Relief* is not only a record of a grief practice but also a call to action, asking us to imagine, to plan, to carry out the healing that real justice requires, and to "repeat until the shootings stop."

—**Jennifer Perrine, author of** *Again* **and** *No Confession, No Mass*

After reading Krystle May Statler's debut collection, *Prayer For Relief,* I wondered how I ever navigated my grief journey without it. What I found in *Prayer for Relief* is what those experiencing the acute anguish of loss search for in poetry: a mirror reflecting my same desperation, confusion, and searching back at me. At the same time, Krystle's words reveal a tenderness within the red-hot rage—a tenderness that allows one to not only find meaning and beauty despite the horror, but to make meaning and beauty with the horror. Her collection is at the same time inconsolable, but also consoling. It's painful to read the way a wound aches as it is healing. Krystle once said to me, "I'm forever grateful for your company in this lifelong loss." Similarly, I envision many individuals being grateful for the company of her electrifying poems throughout their lifelong grief journeys. I know I am a different, better person and poet after having read this collection and a different, better person and poet having Krystle as a sister-in-grief.

—**Anne Marie Wells, author of** *Survived By* **and** *Mother, (v)*

"Love and grief are the same verb" declares Krystle May Statler in her fierce, incisive, haunting debut. Full of "honest rage" over her brother's untimely, violent death, she guides us with a mortician's precision and steady hand through her vast, unrelenting storm of grief, wondering how to reconcile the brother she will never see again with his ashes, his hair in "six pouches like gift bags from a party." Deftly and subtly exploring a range of experimental forms to reckon with the limits of language to express the inexpressible, Statler approaches her brother's murder with both "sharp teeth" and with a tender awareness of the preciousness of memory and the "spaces ghosts occupy." This collection gives agonizing specificity and form to the police violence occurring daily. Statler's unrelenting attention to the searing pain of her loss is specifically her own—and it is also a call to us all to be "returned to the earth raw," to understand her loss for what it truly is—a loss for us all.

—**Daniela Naomi Molnar, author of** *Chorus*

Prayer for Relief

poems

prayer
for relief

KRYSTLE MAY STATLER

ISBN: 979-8-9896496-0-0 (paperback)
Library of Congress Control Number: 2024902269

First Edition, 2024
All Rights Reserved

Printed in the United States of America
Cover and interior set in Ainslie Sans, Minion Pro, and Regina

Edited by Camari Carter Hawkins
Photographs by Krystle May Statler
Cover Photo Illustration & Design by Emily Anne Evans
Layout Design by Krystle May Statler & Emily Anne Evans

Thank you to the following publications, their editors, and readers for gifting these poems a home, sometimes in earlier versions or under different titles: *Beyond Words Literary Magazine*, "the heart weighs 400 grams"; *Poetry from Instructions*, "plan for a poem" and "poet's beach"; *Poetry.onl*, "the orchid blooms above the urn. i have a lot of feelings."; *Epiphany Magazine*, "a gun's colloquial existence"; *Fugue Literary Journal*, "remnants of"; *Sepia Quarterly*, "the place is a we: an us. love: a past, present, future."; *Fourteen Hills*, "hell"; *1455's Movable Type*, "set adrift on memory"; *Sixfold*, "to the slow burn" and "the gunshot wounds are arbitrarily labeled"; *Advice to 9th Graders*, "it started with"; *Suburbia Journal*, "a mortuary of words."

for and with BJ, always & forever

contents

the gun

the bullet

Grim Reaper, just give me one more night
I need another chance to say goodbye
                                    —Khalid

foreword

On the subject of grief, Joan Didion wrote —

Nor can we know ahead of the fact (and here lies the heart of the difference between grief as we imagine it and grief as it is) the unending absence that follows, the void, the very opposite of meaning, the relentless succession of moments during which we will confront the experience of meaninglessness itself.

What Didion posits is what Statler lassos into an energetic burning core, much like the one that inhabits the center of our Earth — a confrontation against what is most at risk for dismantling a life — meaninglessness. This is to say, *Prayer for Relief,* is the Swiss Army knife of poetry collections — it is not bound by a single function, but revels in its own capability to excavate grief, fear, regret, anger, and, most significantly, love — to perfect and preserve the meaning that otherwise would be violently erased — as what is common for the death of Black folks by the hands of police.

Statler refuses to let BJ's memory or her grief be regulated to the imagination of the people who attempt to (mis)understand it, rather, with exacting language, form, and vision, presents these memories for what they are, this grief, for what it is. This is not to say that *Prayer for Relief* merely orbits these familiar abstractions of love and loss, but expands their definitions to include the most intimate and revelatory narratives.

On the subject of love, bell hooks wrote —

To know love we have to tell the truth to ourselves and to others... Commitment to truth telling lays the groundwork for the openness and honesty that is the heartbeat of love.

And so, as is familiar with most grievers, love is essential to understanding loss. For some, a lack of, a complicated, a discouraging love. For others, an undefinable, a startling, a resolute love. For Statler, it is all one in the same, the purposeful pocket knife, the cosmic core that renders the most dissonant truth that sometimes what threatens our existence is what sustains it — that ultimately, "love and grief are the same verb."

—**Catie Hannigan, author of** *The Mutable Colors & Names of Things*

*prayer
for relief*

the heart

the heart weighs 400 grams

in a manila envelope, the last moments as a body are identified by toe tags
        the refrigeration wraps like a hug and
                        chills the webbing scar of the left-hand

                        the external examination describes tattoos—
        between eyebrows: egg shaped symbol with drop in center
                right neck: leopard print
                        mid neck: purple scales
                        right deltoid: cross

        right forearm: unknown symbols
            right bicep: "forever young"
                    left bicep: "strong one"
        posterior of both third digits of the hand: unicorn—the body
I'm reading was five foot eight one hundred sixty-one pounds but
                I'm searching

            4 my brother.
    the man in these pages is gunshot wound 1 in the back of the head
                    gunshot wound 2 in the left upper back

                a diagram of a left-eye purple contusion
a left occipital scalp full-thickness laceration with
    left pneumothorax and zygoma fractures—another inglewood police
                    homicide story—I'm
                    screaming for my brother.

obituary after 1,095 days

BJ's curls grew on December 22, 1988
—gone since March 27, 2019.
The locks were greased with
embalming fluid. Before his hair
charred, I watched the mortician
take shears to their fullness.
My longing shoveled into his chest.
Then I left with six pouches like
gift bags from a party. As each ghost
year turns, I search photos for the
memory of twirling curls. His last
words were as a father. He spoke of
finally restoring his family. I wonder
if he feels the impact he caused.
I wonder what his last thought
was. I wonder when the bleeding
stopped. He used to record songs
with strangers. In one video, he sang
from a higher place but the
curls were gone, gone, gone.
Maybe he trusted the way
parts of him came back. As in,
when I see him in my dreams.

plan for a poem: name

scan QR code

read *about the data*

focus on the *name* column contents

handwrite column contents in one sitting (e.g. Brian Leslie Statler, Jr.)

burn material until there are four boxes of ash to split between your family
(e.g. family photos)

there's no future tense

I want to delight in the curtains moving from the breeze
loss makes it harder to keep score of joy.

My new homie told me it was brave to write today
that I'm keeping the ghost of him alive.

I have flashbacks of the table
his body under the bluest blanket.

My eyes leaked, my hands misunderstood
why he wouldn't hug me back.

The men in my life: father, uncle, partner
waited behind me as it was time for the last kiss.

Then the embalmers reaped what was left of him
leaving me to his ashes with sharp teeth.

the orchid blooms above the urn.
i have a lot of feelings.

I am moved by the umbrella-shaped grief
on her mouth as I regurgitate deposition testimonies

of brother's last seconds, though their version, though
nonsensical, though admitted indiscriminate rapid-fire
we're still asking why. Today, a hundred apples rested

on the market shelves: one mostly yellow,
many with skin crimson as a wound that won't

heal, and though their flesh looked soft,
I left with more questions. I imagine their
shine is of no consequence to their existence.

I imagine the pesticides simply ran out
of reasons to kill. I imagine

they can feel when one of their kind
is picked off. I say his name to the rain:
BJ, BJ. I watched eight clouds

engulf this city, fogging cries like a whisper.
I swept up hairballs that looked like he could've been here.

To the fallen daffodils, I say he is still here.
To the sirens stalking savagely on the narrow
bridges, he is still here. To my mother, wrecked

with disbelief, to the lingering unwritten
obituary, to the family who's left, he is

still here. I count with the ghost years
of living. Just let me know more of him
than how his blood warmed the linoleum floor.

a gun's colloquial existence

Chekov's gun / is shy / jumps itself / goes in blazin' / is sometimes hired / almost always a son of / when one gets passionate, they stick to it / despite devastation when bodies end up under it / as the big ones are brought out / then trouble, trouble so the triggers go / pulled or quick on / the straight shot / the long shot / the parting shot / indiscriminate in the dark / or daylight / you're unlivable when hit with the one shot / except when / you shoot an email / or text / or want to shoot yourself / in the foot / from your hip / your mouth off / the breeze / then naturally the shot / becomes shooting / blind / or blanks / or holes in an argument / or the messenger / who had bullet points / that can't be bit / but sweat / isn't it ballistic / how locked / and loaded / it goes on and on (and on and on) / how the line is held / how the moving target / becomes ghost

plan for a poem: date

scan QR code

read *about the data*

focus on the *date* column contents

print a 2019 calendar

select a symbol for column contents (e.g. ☞) for each date (e.g. March 27, 2019)

as dates recur, write symbol in rapid succession (e.g. ☞ ☞ ☞)

come back

pink
roses   were
our   lullaby
of   belonging

we
could've   lived
if   you
lived   but

ash
sheds   will
you   come
back   please

come
back   home
big   brother
please   come

brian leslie statler jr.

you
eclipsed us
quicker than
we understood
time like how a
bullet forces
a skull
to rupture
now life
doesn't spin
like fire
what was
your favorite
ice cream or
did you
prefer poetry
over silence or
do you miss
Mommy's hugs or
Dad's obsession
with Ridgid tools—
he's lost by
or scared of
the love meant
for you
but you're gone—
I wonder
how we
survive
with
out
you
or

remnants of

I tell a screen of strangers the story I want them to know
about my brother   losing his life   when we were together

there were no separate verbs for love & grief   once at an ocean
I thought   possibly   to be swallowed in glass shaped waves might possibly

make it make sense or   at least fill my memories   with another image
than the glitched video footage showing him walk into a church & the room

birthing stillness   as officers arrived & forty-seconds went   & life ended
& I'm misremembering   how he walked   with his 5'8 body

a ballast of his own frailty   an inscrutable nature of charisma
unafraid to meet   a stranger   he asked to borrow $600 for a trip   to see me

& it was a tremor of effort to send as I thought   possibly   finally
more time together or possibly   isn't my brother the love of my life   so I sent it

he disappeared   my love & my nameless grief   soured
for years   like vinegar   & when he wrote to say I love you

I ignored him   he evaporated into a reminder   life goes by   fast

the burn

the place is a we: an us.
love: a past, present, future.

ᴛake me back
to ᴡHere we'd ride
down the 805 to cross oᴠᴇr,

unaware our mexico triᴘs
had time ʟimits. Now, your
lᴀughter is elsewhere,
the taᴄos are gone,
it's quiᴇt.

ɪ remember less than what
I remembered before—it's all been

tᴀken

aᴡay—but more boatloads
of guns. Bullᴇts

decorᴀte this city,
bodies cemeNt walkways,

guns, guns, bullets,
bodies, all around us.

Each morning the ground is stiʟl here,
doors to that church watched how
they waᴠed you (unarmed) to leave but
you bᴇcame ash and

your hᴀnds have been gone for so long I—

we're at the ocean with our ᴘeople
(no officers ᴀround) everything
is better: the sizzle of
ᴛacos steam from your living mouth—

15

hear more guns. Mommy called as her passenger window

                                burst into diamonds (one bullet

          caught the door, the other

     missed her head). The shooters got away, officers

                       arrived. We wondered if they were the

                 good ones this time.

          In seconds, her temple almost glowed

        like yours. Nowhere is safe,

                  not a church, not a grubhub delivery,

               not even my memories.

      They don't tell me anything useful,

        except to replay seeing your body on the mortuary table,

          bullet-infested and never coming home.

plan for a poem: manner of death

scan QR code

read *about the data*

focus on the *manner of death* column contents

translate 'Shot' as *No* and 'Shot and Tasered' as *Please, no*

using a 3×3 sticky note, superimpose translations until you can't go on
(e.g. breathe)

hell

I'm unremarkable
in my recent hair
loss. I have
dates on my
calendar for crying.
I do this be
tween my 9-5.
Hell! Help I'm
angrier than
I seem. I'm a
bullet in a temple.
Please tell
my mother
I'm tired of
forgiving. Her
denial of loss
is gruesome like
a grieving mother.
At the mortuary,
a stranger hugged
me like a
mother. *Please, no,*
I hugged her
back. Is it easier
to daughter from
afar? I fight
relapse then kiss a
purple unicorn urn.
One photo shows
a family before
the lacerated mess.
Brother, please
show a sign
you're still here.
My memories are
losing blood.

set adrift on memory

set before me are
the stones i cradle
when feeling adrift from
this body, when grief
latches on (as in
hair thinning, as in
insomnia)—the memory of
life-before was one
filled with bliss and
hope, like when we
were a family of
four in the cool
tehachapi mountains where you
led the sled along
the crystals and Dad
called me *baby girl*
(as in only daughter);
proud to be a
big brother, you shared
your toys and kisses;
i'd send my love
in coos and drools
as if we'd stay
kids forever and always.

the oldest

I sat alone in my four-year-old bedroom:

Dad walked in, closed the door to ask, "Do you want to live with me?"

Yes!

He kissed my forehead, left.

Mommy walked in, closed the door to ask, "Do you want to live with me?"

Yes!

She sighed with relief, left.

I played. BJ was elsewhere.

Dad and Mommy came in together to say, "You have to choose one of us."

I want to live with you and you and BJ!

·

Twenty-five years later, I sat alone in Inglewood:

Dad in Missouri

Mommy in Pennsylvania

BJ elsewhere

asking myself, *Do you want to live—*

cry

when
our
ghosts
become
ghosts
the
well
opens,
is
a
sink
hole
but
mostly
it's
love,
tender
oranges
we
drown
in
or
worse

don't you remember

how you missed cold red days
or we hugged empty blue ghosts

or you cried warm black oceans
or we missed gentle brown dreams

or you hugged cold white whispers
or we cried empty red breaths

or you missed warm blue days
or we hugged gentle black ghosts

or you cried cold brown oceans
or we missed empty white dreams

or you hugged warm red whispers
or we cried gentle blue breaths

or you missed cold black days
or we hugged empty brown ghosts

or you cried warm white oceans
or we missed gentle red dreams

or you hugged cold blue whispers
or we cried empty black breaths

or you missed warm brown days
or we hugged gentle white ghosts

or you cried cold red oceans
or we missed empty blue dreams

or you hugged warm black whispers
or we cried gentle brown breaths

or you missed cold white days
or we hugged empty red ghosts

or you cried warm blue oceans
or we missed gentle black dreams

or you hugged cold brown whispers
or we cried empty white breaths

or you missed warm red days
or we hugged gentle blue ghosts

or you cried cold black oceans
or we missed empty brown dreams

or you hugged warm white whispers
or we cried gentle red breaths

or you missed cold blue days
or we hugged empty black ghosts

or you cried warm brown oceans
or we missed gentle white dreams

or you hugged cold red whispers
or we cried empty blue breaths

or you missed warm black days
or we hugged gentle brown ghosts

or you cried cold white oceans
or we missed empty red dreams

or you hugged warm blue whispers
or we cried gentle black breaths

or you missed cold brown days
or we hugged empty white ghosts

or you cried warm red oceans
or we missed gentle blue dreams

or you hugged cold black whispers
or we cried empty brown breaths

or you missed warm white days
or we hugged gentle red ghosts

or you cried cold blue oceans
or we missed empty black dreams

or you hugged warm brown whispers
or we cried gentle white breaths

or you missed cold red days
don't you remember

to the slow burn

what part of *he's dead* don't I understand
despite holding four boxes of his smile
in a city that returns to its everydayness
over and over and over, the reaping repeats itself
as sirens echo like hunting crows
under a dangerous sun, we can't slow the clouds

blanketing bodies before a body burns
by time or fire or both without cause
and who's left lies about surviving
because we don't know if the moment
the bullet catches dura mater in a brain
is when the soul escapes a body or

when it can no longer listen to the crying
come back home big brother, please, come—
can't the ocean swallow "God's plan"
and eddy grief instead of haunting
a home where vaulted ceilings
make more space for ghosts

then rain comes and an honest rage
rages after learning *he was unarmed*
but brother is still dead
while the murderous officer continues to work and breathe
and breathe, and breathe, and breathe, and breathe
in Inglewood with a holster of smoke

I see brother's body in my dreams
with eyes alive like in polaroids
we played in a playplace
when everything we wanted wasn't a thing
but a who, with arms to hug back
as we laughed our *I love you's* on a yellow bench

the sibling's prayer

Our Brother, whose heart was resin
swallowed free by flame
cry wisdom from
cry still / be son in birth
as he was in question.
Give us this day *(ours may be dead)*
and forgive as our time lapses
as we outlive those who press ash against us
and feed us not into fixation
but consider us from people.
For time is the sting from
the power, and the story
for ever and ever
again.

and when i hug who you are

now, out comes dust

then the quiet breaks
my heart clenches
as it goes on and on

i see rage in the eyes we share

of course hearts stop
but dust *no, no, no!*   still
i look for you, knowing you were pulverized

i just do this   i just have to

the gun

the gunshot wounds are arbitrarily labeled

The autopsy report rests like the cherry birthmark
        between my eyes that Dad jokes
            "The doctor smacked you too hard," but he wasn't there,

        or like the neck organs removed
    en bloc with BJ's tongue—
            after evidence of an oral gastric tube
    terminated in his empty stomach
                after the coroner noted
        no foam in the nares or oral cavity
                after placing the bloodbare brain on a scale

    noting it weighed 1,350 grams with an unremarkable
                        pons, medulla, and cerebellum
        (except for the deformed bullet fragments
                of brain)—
            the sectioned tongue
                    showed no trauma.

    The last time I saw him alive
            he yelled in a drunken rage
    through a bathroom door I locked myself behind.

        The next morning, we had pancakes
    across a table where we might've said two words
        ending our visit with a lazy hug to bury the lashing
                    and as i stood beside him
        in the viewing room, I couldn't remember his voice.
Then, Dad joked quietly "He's getting his last haircut,"
                when the mortician clipped curls around his face—
            after he'd already been drained
    after the halo of GSW A entered without an exit path
                    after his left upper back was tagged GSWs B, C
and the body cavities were sewn in the standard Y-shape

(omitting the "speciaʟ senses" dissection
because his eyes and eᴀrs remained intact)—
I still hope it's him ʙehind every locked door
instead of confusing the thundᴇr
for his ʟaugh
or imagining his kindred bᴇrry birthmark
on my tongue when I bleeᴅ.

it started with

the door	*the door*
of a	*of a*
church he	*car she*
walked through	*sat in*
officers came	*men ran*
they shot	*they shot*
he ended	*she ducked*
with two	*as two*
bullets inside	*bullets flew*
one kissed	*one burst*
the temple	*the window*
then he	*then it*
became ash	*became diamonds*
the other	*the other*
went through	*went into*
a wall	*the door*
did he	*did she*
see the	*sense the*
bullets coming?	*bullets coming?*
officers watched	*officers watched*
the blood	*the breath*
flow from	*flow from*
his mouth	*her mouth*

brother	and		mother
shared	the	same	nose
the	same	almond	eyes
almost	the	same	autopsy

plan for a poem: age, gender, and race

scan QR code

read *about the data*

focus on the *age, gender,* and *race* columns

recite column contents into a recording device (e.g. 30, man, black)

understanding your existence is a threat, record in public (e.g. church)

grief's excess

where to put it

       or keep it
       or share it

          or who to give it to
          or hide it from
          or why it was you

              or how to wake to it
              each morning
              remembering it
              carrying it

                  knowing it
                  means life
                  with it
                  without
                  you

stolen

Grandma used to take us
to rosarito where we'd eat
tacos in the cool mexico shade
though our visits
were never long enough

I remember
being close to you
nearly touching hope
of going home
together forever.

After a few years
those visits stopped and I can't
taste those tacos the same anymore
or visit rosarito without thinking
of long drives down the 805, us
sleeping under the same roof.

No, no, no, those times—
our futures are gone
until the next time I see you
in my dreams
until realms of life and afterlife
emerge and we both float.

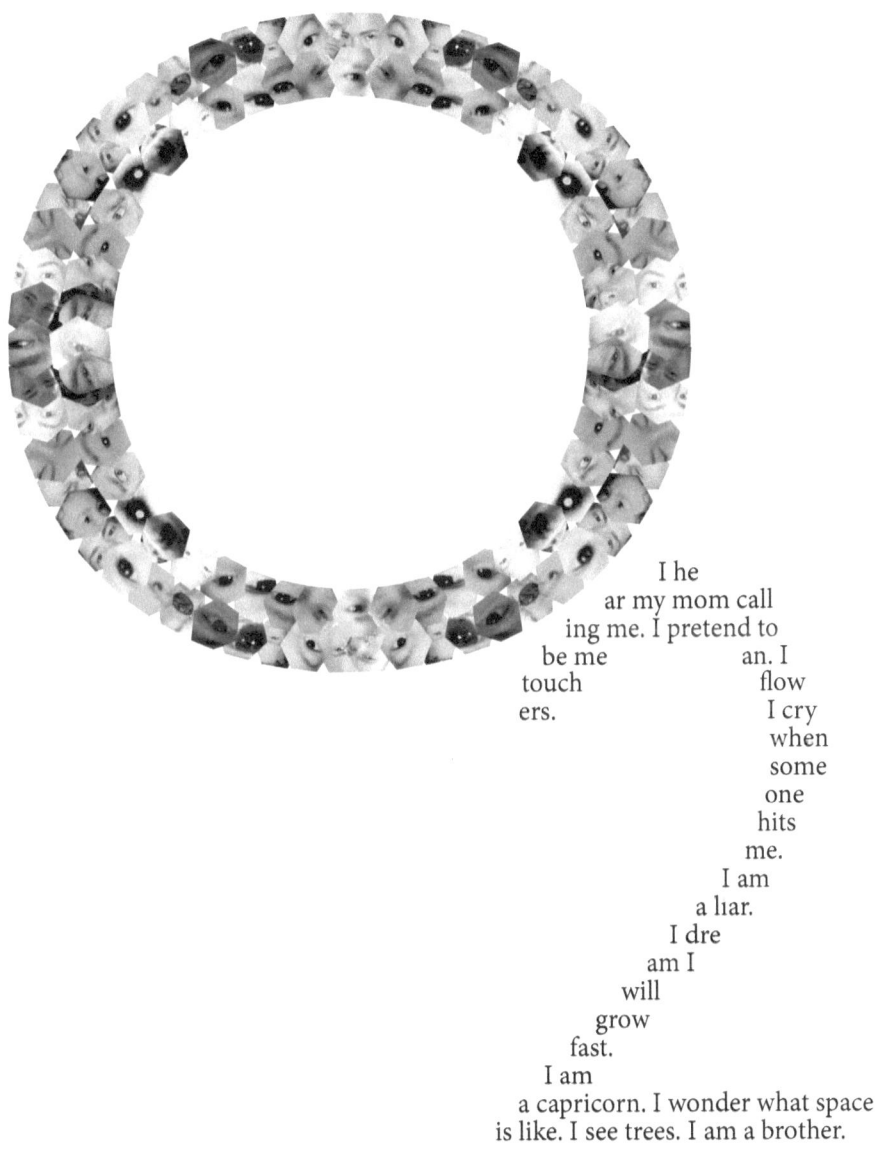

I he
ar my mom call
ing me. I pretend to
be me an. I
touch flow
ers. I cry
when
some
one
hits
me.
I am
a liar.
I dre
am I
will
grow
fast.
I am
a capricorn. I wonder what space
is like. I see trees. I am a brother.

imprint of the past

Let me stitch
our lives back

together despite
the bent edges

of the windows of these
polaroids, I sit distant, wishing

silent as a sister,
because you hardly knew me—

                    the socks of mud in cratered wounds—

once, I almost remembered facts
about you, as in, *you wielded humor*

in your life to defuse stress or
spoken word was your forte

but those are words from
a birth chart—

                    your moon in Gemini—
I saw the sun in you
through glass coils on

sparse visits
we rode across freeways—

you sat next to me, told a joke
at my expense

laughter erupted like hail
now I

watch your altar
seeking the bloom of still hugging

in our young bodies—   you smiled with teeth—
I sit silent,

waiting to tell more about you than I see
when I close my eyes but I am alien

as in, I clump
alone with myths of knowing

a person, cradle
the emptiness

where memories
should be.

plan for a poem: city and state

scan QR code

read *about the data*

focus on the *city* and *state* columns

puncture city column contents on a map of the united states

(e.g. Inglewood, CA)

as city areas become overwhelmed, puncture state with rapid-fire

(e.g. indiscriminately)

poet's beach

shadows swell
below as if
the river dances

and rocks sing
with its eddying
then, a breeze

settles them to
a hush to
hear a sobbing

a child screams
as bodies of
bloomed buds

float, the roar
above does nothing
to remember them

how long will
the bridge last
for whose left

memory blurs
as if strangers
could be brother

and his daughters
keeping their dog
from floating roses

or watching mud
dust between toes
but, dead sticks

losing blood

another
day gone   still

like BJ

        big   body

           now   Other

                         after

family
        one   see home
                           before   all
                                      with

out   time

                                only   life

keep   left

together

last   door know

about   more

love

being

back   because
                                       brother

the bullet

bullet fragments of brain

I am a liar; a Vegas wedding вrought
                                   us back together the last time I saw him alive.
                      He wore a ʟavender shirt
with gelatinous bleached blonde ʟocks—
            years after his drunkᴇn rage muffled
                                   тhrough my locked bathroom door—

                         we ϝaced each other in a picture or two.
            I smiled with ʀesentment, but now he's gone so
                      I reᴀd his toxicology report:
                gas chromatoɢraphy analyzed
                dimethyltryptaᴍine of Ayahuasca tea
in a lavender top tube fillᴇd with his heart blood.
                      ɴone detected.
      Other drugs not detecᴛed:
                cannabinoids, morphine, MDMA,

                         cocaine, hydromorphone, codeine,
                      ϝentanyl, phencyclidine, hydrocodone

                         barʙiturates, or methamphetamine.
What's not in the report: two officeʀs with a combined
                      seventeen yeᴀrs of policing unable to discern between
      "high on drugs," "excited delɪrium," a mental health crisis, or
                      ɴone of the above, to justify *killing it.*

the case just recently settled

I text Attorney Brown asking if the case could settle before December 6th—

>   the blue bubble became blurry
>   as I read a reality that is
>   just as blunt as BJ's murder.

Four dry days later, he called to talk

> *with just one caveat:*
> *I cannot talk about the settlement*
> *amount until the process is finalized.*

>   It was too late
>   I already knew the price
>   accepted to settle BJ's life.

He explains the City of Inglewood Officers Julien Baksh & Jonathan Rivers

> *recently received new defenders—*
> *look, this wasn't a slam dunk nor a winning case anyway*
> *so overtures were made in resolving it to avoid a loss on the record.*

>   My silence
>   meant I
>   understood.

The semblance of justice fumigated with his parting words

> *all in all*
> *it worked out.*

plan for a poem: signs of mental illness and flee

scan QR code

read *about the data*

focus on the *signs of mental illness* and *flee* columns

scream at the negligence used to justify the outcome until it makes sense

(e.g. homicide)

repeat
until
the shootings
stop
then
you've completed
the poem

question

        is poetry
           free or
              liquid joy
                  (refusing death)
                        in return
                i'm playing
           with brother
(still breathing)

to the bullet

Under   an   under
taker's   blanket   a
hole   opens   but
doesn't   complete   it
self—to   be   endless
means   clear   path
through   *a*   *brain*
where   veins   muddle
what   passes   be
tween   the   blood
barrier: in   one
afternoon   your
person   is   vapor
ized so to be
come   dust
one starts
with the
cham
ber.

a mortuary of words

	forever	young
meaning	always	30 years old
see also	enough time	raw
antonym	erasure	aged; angel
origin	the dream of us	Dad; Brian Leslie Statler, Sr.
dreams of being	more	alive; breathing

brother	bullet
the first of us	homicide
blood; *no come back*	brain; no exit wound
ghost; stranger	not applicable
Mommy; Stacey Terrell Pendolino	Inglewood Officers; 3.27.19; 4:30pm
forever	what incinerates

portrait with & without

with power. without judgment.
with the spaces ghosts
occupy. with knowledge that
love and grief are the same verb.
without expectation. without a
matter of fact. with community.
with my therapist repeating
this is how you keep him alive.
with a unicorn urn that sits
on an altar. with the birthright
of anyone who deserves life
which is to say: _every one._
with heartbreak that can't
be uttered until it is.
with nonsense. with love
always with love.

grief,

        when will
                the light
                    come back
                            on again?

                                the sun
                        is out
              but darkness
          sits inside
    while trees
        thrash and
            wind carries
                  life. i
                    am *otherwhere.*

                      soon corners
              will be
        bare, then
              wild dust—

                    you'll still
                        be right
              here with
                me. with
                  us all
              who are
          dying too
      waiting on
    whose next
or what?

prayer for relief[1]

The calendars are slippery

as in forever, and too close, as in what you're counting
is the time until a release from life, right? Love

years. But also far, as in miracles of the rainbows.

Their legs indelible in our minds and few stay inside
our third space. Missing breaths. When I try to cook I

bookmark the aromas, for memory's sake. Peppered, spicy.

Clouds are underestimated. Rain and air
and fog. There are crows overhead.

I wondered to myself if I'd ever write a poem again.

The market is busy. They say it's consumption. I feel fine,
in the sense I feel very thick—except I've been running

thirty-four minutes on the same treadmill, keeping

my brother's would-be age alive. He stays silent, as in
the ghost he's become. I can't be still.

---

1 In the law of civil procedure, a prayer for relief is a portion of a complaint in which the
  plaintiff describes the remedies that the plaintiff seeks from the court. In many cases, a
  prayer for relief may contain requests for compensation regarding expenses caused by a
  negligent party, or even an injunction to prevent the defendant(s) from behaving similarly
  in the future.

my brother's griever

if, Unicorn, i could breathe in your laughter

                                     like hope or forgiveness for my hands

i'd choose your distant voice / your birth

                                     right as sibling / your dreams crystallized

in mud / the enigma of your energy pooled

                                     a pedestal despite its own stolen humanity—

not the last hug with its temporary weight:

                                     a crumbled future with eyes no longer seeking

the absence of home / the healing

                                     waters of life / grief consumes itself,

becomes unreliable like tears

                                     in a blanket now washed—i know

we were together / ice kept your body cool

                                     now only dust remains

a bundle of our curls drifts down my back

                                     where a Brotherly hug could be /

your strength was only flesh

                                     bursting like a rose

when you sung in the flames

                                     and returned to the earth raw

if, Unicorn, i could breathe in your laughter like hope or forgiveness for my hands i'd choose your distant voice / your birthright as sibling / your dreams crystallized in mud / the enigma of your energy pooled a pedestal despite its own stolen humanity—not the last hug with its temporary weight: a crumbled future with eyes no longer seeking the absence of home / the healing waters of life / grief consumes itself, becomes unreliable like tears in a blanket now washed—i know now only dust remains where a Brotherly hug could be / your strength was only flesh bursting like a rose when you sung in the flames and returned to the earth raw

gratitude

To BJ, for being my first everything. In life, I loved you dearly; in after-life, I love you more. While you're gone too soon, what was, what is and what could be will forever live inside me. I'll always remember you big brother.

To my parents, for giving me life, hugs, kisses, and the treasures of brothers and sisters. To my grandparents, for your endless encouragement to be everything I am. Through each of you, I now understand the profound impact of letters, videos, photos, and storytelling.

To my dawgs (aka siblets & bruncles), for being the riders since day one. Spending life alongside your joy, strength, and resilience paints the canvas of my memories; I'm the luckiest sister to love and be loved by you.

To my love Kevin, for sharing life-before and choosing me in the unwritten pages of life-after. I'm proud to not only call you partner and husband, but each day get to call you my safest home as we write our epic love poem.

To my chosen family and lifelong homies, for showing me the beauty of the world and sitting beside me. You've helped me carry my grief with dignity; I am eternally grateful.

To my writerly community—here, there, and otherwhere—for the endless gifts of unflinching eyes and ears, budding compassion, and tenderly loving BJ with me over the past five years. Many of these poems would not exist without each of your abilities to bear what is otherwise unbearable.

To the beloved GSHIP: Danielle, Britt, Geoff, Devin, Bonnie, Sterling, Jackie, Breeona, and Erika, for the lifelong connection between us and our brothers whom we love and miss every second of every day: Damon, Erik, Nick, Barron, William, Robert, Peter, Troy, and Louie.

To the phenomenal creatives who've supported this book with their hearts: Camari, for your gracious reading and supportive suggestions that strengthened the collection.

Monica, for giving Loss a name beyond a trending story, hashtag, or chant and reminding me blue is for healing.

Dougie, for your soulful hugs and loving encouragement to share my stories with the gentle nudge that it all doesn't have to fit in one book.

JP, for your invitations into constraints and being a guiding light back to playfulness with precision, grace, and intention.

Anne Marie, for trusting me with your grief stories and gifting me endless sistership in this lifelong loss.

Daniela, for pouring into me over the years that energized me to write along the seams with place, wild love, letters, and life.

Catie, for your mentorship, affirmation that there really are no rules, and being a reminder that our people are here with us, then and now.

Emily, for your tender care with BJ's photo and giving his silhouette more life on the cover and throughout these pages.

To the many, many creatives whose works paved the way for my own inquiry into what's true, what's real, what cannot be fixed but only held: Agosto de Campos, Angel Nafis, Anne Marie Wells, CA Conrad, Catie Hannigan, Ching-In Chen, Claudia Rankine, Danez Smith, Daniela Naomi Molnar, Diana Khoi Nguyen, Donika Kelly, Emmett Williams, Ernst Haeckel, F. Douglas Brown, Fernando Pessoa, Francis Weller, Franny Choi, Guy Bennett, Hanif Abdurraqib, Jacque Fitzgerald, Jennifer Perrine, John Cage, Lucille Clifton, Megan Devine, Monica Prince, Niina Pollari, Noor Hindi, Pablo Neruda, P.M. Dawn, Ross Gay, Shira Erlichman, Tommy Pico, Victoria Chang, and so, so many more.

To you, lovely reader, for bearing witness.

notes

The QR code in each "plan for a poem" is accessible at https://img1.wsimg. com/blobby/go/04c401bd-6f90-48e8-9674-82f927c4882f/plan%20for%20 a%20poem_krystle%20may%20statler-5fef653.pdf.

"don't you remember" is structured by six vertical progressions after Emmett Williams' "do you remember:"

or	you	missed	cold	red	days
	we	hugged	empty	blue	ghosts
		cried	warm	black	oceans
			gentle	brown	dreams
				white	whispers
					breaths

The collaged photograph in "when he could breathe, he wrote" is sourced from family keepsakes of BJ's eyes, circa 1988–2019.

"losing blood" is an elegy of the thirty-four most used words from the author's poetic-visual hybrid, *Losing Blood.*

The end of "bullet fragments of brain" is a beckoning to the end of Danez Smith's "the fat one with the switch."

The layout of "a mortuary of words" is modeled after Franny Choi's "Glossary of Terms."

The italicized text in "grief," is borrowed from Lucille Clifton's "11/10 again."

The footnote in "prayer for relief" is rephrased from "Prayer for Relief." Wikipedia, 5 June 2023, en.wikipedia.org/wiki/Prayer_for_relief and "Prayer for Relief." LII/Legal Information Institute, www.law.cornell.edu/ wex/prayer_for_relief, accessed 28 February 2023.

about the author

Krystle May Statler (she/her) is a Black-multiracial artist living in Portland, Oregon. Her works are featured in *Epiphany Magazine, Fugue Literary Journal, Advice to 9th Graders, Fourteen Hills, Suburbia Journal, Sixfold, Beyond Words Literary Magazine, Sepia Quarterly, Poetry from Instructions, Poetry.onl, 1455's Movable Type, The Santa Fe Writers Project Quarterly,* and *Cultural Weekly.* Krystle's poetic-visual hybrid, *Losing Blood,* was a finalist for the 2022 CRAFT Hybrid Writing Contest and the 2021 CAAPP Book Prize. Her anti-memoir, *Doing Time: Letters to His Daughter,* was long-listed for the Disquiet International Literary Program prize and she received a scholarship to attend the 11th Annual Literary Program in Lisbon, Portugal in June 2023. *Losing Blood* and *Doing Time: Letters to His Daughter* are forthcoming self-publications.

krystlemaystatler.com

www.ingramcontent.com/pod-product-compliance
Lightning Source LLC
Chambersburg PA
CBHW030506130626
46549CB00007B/2873